PowerKiDS
Readers

Happy Holidays!
¡Felices Fiestas!

St. Patrick's Day
Día de San Patricio

Josie Keogh

Traducción al español:
Eduardo Alamán

PowerKiDS
press™

New York

For the Beirne family

Published in 2013 by The Rosen Publishing Group, Inc.
29 East 21st Street, New York, NY 10010

First Edition

Traducción al español: Eduardo Alamán

Editor: Amelie von Zumbusch
Book Design: Andrew Povolny

Photo Credits: Cover R. Nelson/Flickr/Getty Images; pp. 5, 17 © iStockphoto.com/Liza McCorkle; p. 7 Martin Gray/National Geographic/Getty Images; p. 9 Time Life Pictures/Getty Images; p. 11 Terrie L. Zeller/Shutterstock.com; p. 13 KidStock/Blend Images/Getty Images; p. 15 Ken Ilio/Flickr/Getty Images; p. 19 Goodshoot/Thinkstock; p. 21 Stuart Monk/Shutterstock.com; p. 23 Vsevolod33/Shutterstock.com.

Library of Congress Cataloging-in-Publication Data

Keogh, Josie.
 St. Patrick's Day = Día de San Patricio / by Josie Keogh ; translated by Eduardo Alamán. — 1st ed.
   p. cm. — (Powerkids readers: happy holidays! / ¡Felices Fiestas!)
 Includes index.
 ISBN 978-1-4488-9971-5 (library binding)
 1. Saint Patrick's Day—Juvenile literature. I. Alamán, Eduardo. II. Title.
 GT4995.P3K46 2013
 394.262—dc23
                         2012022318

Websites: Due to the changing nature of Internet links, PowerKids Press has developed an online list of websites related to the subject of this book. This site is updated regularly. Please use this link to access the list: www.powerkidslinks.com/pkrhh/stpa/

Manufactured in the United States of America

CPSIA Compliance Information: Batch #W13PK3: For Further Information contact Rosen Publishing, New York, New York at 1-800-237-9932

Contents

Contenido

It is St. Patrick's Day!

¡Es Día de San Patricio!

Patrick was an Irish saint.

Patricio fue un santo irlandés.

He was born in Britain.

Nació en la Gran Bretaña.

PATRICK

9

Draw a **shamrock**.

Dibuja un **trébol**.

Eat a treat!

¡Come algo rico!

The Chicago River gets
dyed green!

¡En Chicago, el río Chicago se
tiñe de verde!

15

Green stands for Ireland.

El color verde representa
a Irlanda.

Eire is the Irish name
for Ireland.

El nombre de Irlanda, en el
idioma irlandés, es Éire.

19

New York has the biggest **parade**.

En Nueva York se realiza el **desfile** de San Patricio más grande.

20

21

A **step dance** competition is a feis.

El **zapateado** es una competición de danza en el festival llamado *feis*.

WORDS TO KNOW / PALABRAS QUE DEBES SABER

parade

(el) desfile

shamrock

(el) trébol

step dance

(el) zapateado

24